YOUR KNOWLEDGE HAS

Bibliographic information published by the German National Library:

The German National Library lists this publication in the National Bibliography; detailed bibliographic data are available on the Internet at http://dnb.dnb.de .

Imprint:

Copyright © 2017 GRIN Verlag
Print and binding: Books on Demand GmbH, Norderstedt Germany
ISBN: 9783668660618

This book at GRIN:

https://www.grin.com/document/415839

Nonita Sharma

XGBoost. The Extreme Gradient Boosting for Mining Applications

GRIN Verlag

GRIN - Your knowledge has value

Since its foundation in 1998, GRIN has specialized in publishing academic texts by students, college teachers and other academics as e-book and printed book. The website www.grin.com is an ideal platform for presenting term papers, final papers, scientific essays, dissertations and specialist books.

Visit us on the internet:

http://www.grin.com/

http://www.facebook.com/grincom

http://www.twitter.com/grin_com

Extreme Gradient Boosting for Mining Applications

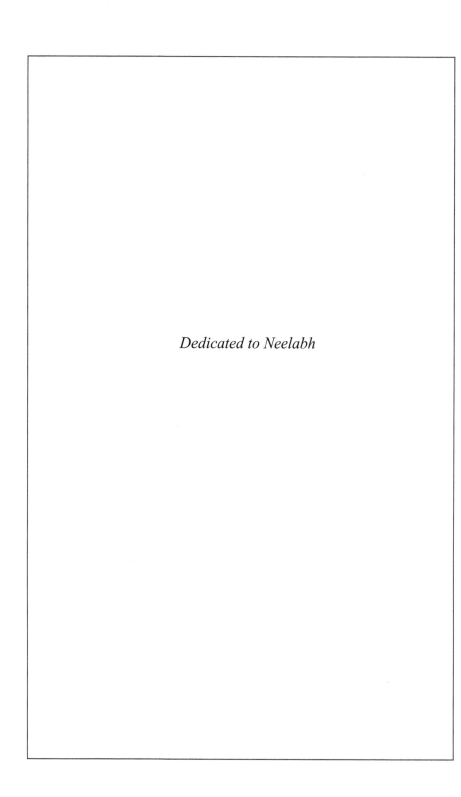

Dedicated to Neelabh

Abstract

Tree boosting has empirically proven to be a highly effective and versatile approach for data-driven modelling. The core argument is that tree boosting can adaptively determine the local neighbourhoods of the model thereby taking the bias-variance trade-off into consideration during model fitting. Recently, a tree boosting method known as XGBoost has gained popularity by providing higher accuracy. XGBoost further introduces some improvements which allow it to deal with the bias-variance trade-off even more carefully. In this research work, we propose to demonstrate the use of an adaptive procedure i.e. Learned Loss(LL) to update the loss function as the boosting proceeds. Accuracy of the proposed algorithm i.e. XGBoost with Learned Loss boosting function is evaluated using test/train method, K-fold cross validation, and Stratified cross validation method and compared with the state of the art algorithms viz. XGBoost, AdaBoost, AdaBoost-NN, Linear Regression(LR),Neural Network(NN), Decision Tree(DT), Support Vector Machine(SVM), bagging-DT, bagging-NN and Random Forest algorithms. The parameters evaluated are accuracy, Type 1 error and Type 2 error (in Percentages). This study uses total ten years of historical data from Jan 2007 to Aug 2017 of two stock market indices CNX Nifty and S&P BSE Sensex which are highly voluminous.

Further, in this research work, we will investigate how XGBoost differs from the more traditional ensemble techniques. Moreover, we will discuss the regularization techniques that these methods offer and the effect these have on the models.

In addition to this, we will attempt to answer the question of why XGBoost seems to win so many competitions. To do this, we will provide some arguments for why tree boosting, and in particular XGBoost, seems to be such a highly effective and versatile approach to predictive modelling. The core argument is that tree boosting can be seen to adaptively determine the local neighbourhoods of the model. Tree boosting can thus be seen to take the bias-variance trade off into consideration during model fitting. XGBoost further introduces some improvements which allow it to deal with the bias-variance trade off even more carefully.

Acknowledgement

I would like to thank first and foremost to God, who has been my strength during my whole life.

Then, I would like to thank my supervisor Prof (Dr) Ajay K Sharma for his guidance, inspiration, encouragement, and demonstrative support throughout this work. Without his continuous and extensive support, this work would never have gone this far.

I wish to thank my parents for their love and encouragement during my whole life. Special mention must be made to my sister and brother-in-law for their never ending support from starting till the end. I would like to express my gratefulness to my friend Akanksha for her invaluable support and encouragement.

Finally, I express my deepest gratitude and appreciation to my husband Neelabh and my daughters Shambhvi and Shreyanvi for their continuous support and understanding during my pursuit that made the completion of book possible. I gratefully dedicate this book to them for their love, care and support.

(Nonita)

Table of Contents

List of Figures

List of Tables

List of Acronyms

AC	Admissibility Criteria
AF	Affinity Function
AS	Agglomerative Scheme
ADA	Algorithm Design & Analysis
AdaBoost	Adaptive Boosting
AoV	Analysis of Variance
AI	Artificial Intelligence
ASE	Average Square Error
BD	Baseline Distribution
BR	Binary Relation
BS	Bootstrap
BT	Box Test
CA	Classification Algorithms
CL	Complete Link
CLJ	Complete Link Johnson's
CM	Computation Modeling
DDP	Distributed Data Processing
DM	Data Mining
DBA	Distributed Boosting Algorithm
DSL	Divisive Single Link
DT	Decision Tree

CHAPTER I
Theoretical Foundations

1.1 Outline

In the course of recent decades, machine learning and data mining have turned out to be one of the backbones of data innovation and with that, a somewhat central, although typically hidden, part of our life. With the constantly expanding amounts of data getting to be noticeably accessible there is justifiable reason to consider that information mining will turn out to be a significant element for technological advancements. Nowadays, machine learning and information mining have turned into a vital piece of human life. In all aspects of life, applications of these two are utilized. Example applications include fraud detection, e-mail protection, in recommender system it helps to find out the user taste product etc. (1).

Further, Boosting is the most widely used tool used in machine learning that improves the accuracy of prediction of various classification models. Boosting technique is an ensemble technique created by combing various weak learners to build a strong learner with higher precision. Weak learners are those indicators that give more precision than random guessing. However, strong learners are those classifiers that give maximum accuracy and hence coined as the base of machine learning. Boosting technique is employed when the dataset is large and high predictive power is the vital requisite of the application. Further, it is also used to reduce the bias and variance in the prediction models. However, the technique also solves the over-fitting problem for smaller dataset. Additionally, it has wide application area and applies on numerous classification techniques viz. feature selection, feature extraction, and multi-class categorization. The applications of boosting include medical area, text classification, page ranking and business and so on (2).

Furthermore, Boosting technique is a type of ensemble method, which is used when there is a collection of many weighted same or different type of predictors. However in this technique, a collection of several hypothesis is selected and eventually their prediction is combined. For example, if 50 decision trees are generated over same or different training data set then a new test dataset is created and voted for best classification.

To illustrate, a simple example of boosting is suppose we have to identify about insurance company i.e. fraud or not and following key points are there:

- Company has a high profit – Strong
- Queries are solved on the toll free number – Weak
- Company has a proper mail id and proper website – Strong
- It gives a proper receipt after paying the amount – Strong
- Large number of customers - Strong
- Behaviour with the customers – Weak

In the above query, there are four strong and two weak points and when we collect all the points. Then according to the majority it can be inferred that the company is not fraud and anyone can invest his money on this. Hence, boosting considers assigning weights to various points and then combining the results to predict the class. In addition, several boosting algorithms are already in place. The most widely used are:

1. Adaptive Boosting (AdaBoost)
2. Gradient Boosting
3. Extreme Gradient Boosting (XGBoost)
4. Random Forest

1.1.1 AdaBoost

AdaBoost also known as Adaptive Boosting algorithm is proposed by Freund and Schapire (5). It is an ensemble learning technique where multiple weak learners are consolidated to create one strong learning algorithm. The algorithm starts by selecting a base classification algorithm (e.g. Naïve Bayes) and repetitively enhancing its prediction accuracy by draining the inaccurately classified samples in the training dataset. Initially, AdaBoost assigns same weights to all the training samples and selects a base classifier algorithm. Further, for every iteration, the base algorithm classifies the training samples and the weights of the inaccurate classified samples are increased. The algorithm iterates n times, repeatedly applying base classification algorithm on the training dataset with new calculated weights. At the end, the final classification model is the weighted sum of the n classifiers (6). Fig. 1 shows the AdaBoost algorithm, where D is the decision tree that is used to classify plus and minus point. Box 4 is the final model that correctly classifies the data points.

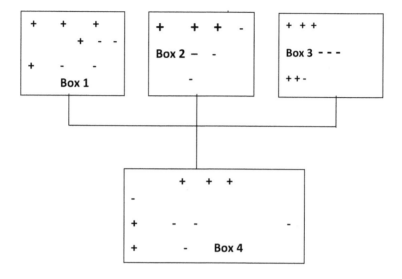

Fig. 1.1 AdaBoost Example

1.1.2 Gradient boosting

Gradient boosting is an effective off-the-shelf strategy for creating accurate models for classification problems. The technique has empirically proven itself to be highly effective for a vast array of classification and regression problems. As stated previously, gradient boosting is a variant of ensemble method, meaning that the prediction is consolidated from several simpler predictors. The aim of this method is to train a collection of decision tress, given the case that the training of single decision tree is known apriori. The technique is called "boosting" in light of the fact that we anticipate that combined results will provide more accuracy than a single learner. However, in this method the boosting is visualized as an optimization problem, where the objective of the technique is to minimize the loss of the classifier model by adding one weak learner at a time as done in a gradient descent. Gradient boosting is also called stage-wise additive classifier as a new weak learner is added at one time and the previously classified weak learners are left frozen i.e. unchanged for that iteration.

1.1.3 XGBoost

XGBoost stands for extreme gradient boosting, developed by Tianqi Chen. Since its introduction in 2014, XGBoost has quickly become among the most popular methods used for classification in machine learning. It is an implementation over the gradient boosting. XGBoost is greedy in nature so it follows greedy approach. It has high performance and speed. XGBoost is a scalable system for learning Tree ensemble method. It is used for wide number of applications and it also supports outdoor memory (3). Due to parallel computation process it is faster than other boosting algorithms (4).The reason behind the higher performance of XGBoost is that it is scalable in nature. Additionally, it has following advantages over other algorithm.

- Due to parallel processing process it has faster performance than gradient boosting.

- It controls the over fitting problem.

- It gives a better performance result on many datasets.

- It is extreme gradient boosting.

- Basically it is a tree building algorithm.

- It is used for classification, regression and ranking with custom loss functions.

1.1.4 Random Forest

Another ensemble technique that is widely used in Machine Learning is random forest. It is used in classification, regression and many more prediction problems. At training time, multiple decision trees are created and the output is the mean or average prediction of each trees. The algorithm is proposed by Tin Kam Ho (7). Random forest follows following steps:

- Using the bagging process sampling of training dataset takes place. It gives a number of trees.

- Nodes are split according to some splitting criteria.

- Due to splitting criteria, data is divided into each node.

- Classification takes place on leaf node.

- After trained for trees, test data is sampled. Each sample is given to all trees.

- At the leaf node classification takes place.

- At last, the class of the test dataset is decided by majority voting or average process.

Furthermore, in random forest algorithm, the classifier shows low bias and high variance. Random Forest follows the parallel computation process. The algorithm that is used for training and testing process is bootstrapping. However, for very iteration, data is split into number of trees using bagging process. Bagging process divides the whole dataset and creates samples. Then, classification is done on these samples using decision trees. Further the classifier predicts the classes of samples and final class is predicted by the majority voting or it can be the simple average. In various situations, Random Forest gives more exact predictions when distinguished with simple Classification and Regression Tree (CART) models or regression models.

1.1.5 Comparison of Boosting Algorithms

XGBoost and its entire variant exhibit the maximal performance among all the categories of boosting algorithms, however AdaBoost displays the minimal performance lower than random forest. This can be attributed to the computation process followed in the respective boosting algorithms. XGBoost and Random forest implement parallel computation process while Adaboost realize serial computation process. Hence, the performance also displays the same realization. In boosting, several weak learners are combined and prediction is given by one strong learner. The final prediction can hence, be made by weighted average or simple average of weak learners. In weighted average, more weight is given to a learner with higher classification accuracy. On the other hand, no weights are allocated to the weak learners in simple average. XGBoost and AdaBoost use the concept of weighted average while random forest consider the simple average of weak learners.

Further, in boosting various weak learners are consolidated and give a strong learner with higher accuracy. Therefore, bias and variance are considered important parameters to measure the accuracy of these algorithms. The better algorithm is the one which provides high bias and low variance. Both XGBoost and AdaBoost depict the same. But Random forest shows the opposite. Accuracy is also impacted by the cross validation of error. All the four algorithms implement the cross validation of error and hence are more accurate than single learner. To state the comparative analysis of the accuracy of all the four algorithms, accuracy of XGBoost is maximum and random forest shows the least accuracy amongst all. Over fitting of data occurs due to the branches involving noisy data or outliers. It is imperative to reduce the over fitting problem to enhance the accuracy of the learners. Pruning is done to remove the over fitting of data. The pruning can be done in two ways: Pre-pruning and post-pruning. Pre-pruning involves the avoidance of over fitting problem while post pruning removes the overfitted data after the learner is created. XGBoost and Random Forest avoids over fitting problem, Adaboost does not avoid the problem completely but it is less prone to over fitting.

In summary, XGBoost which is implemented on gradient boosting algorithm and follows the greedy approach is the best performing boosting algorithm in terms of computation performance and accuracy. A comparative analysis between the techniques is demonstrated in Table 1.1.

Table 1.1: Comparative Evaluation of Boosting Algorithms

Technique	Computation Process	Final Prediction	Training & Testing Algorithm	Bias	Variance
XGBoost	Parallel	Weighted Average	Any Algorithm can be used	High	Low
AdaBoost	Serial	Weighted Average	Any Algorithm can be used	High	Low
Random Forest	Parallel	Simple Average	Bootstrapping	Low	High

1.1.6 Loss Functions in Boosting Algorithms

Every learning issue has a particular learning objective that have to achieve. A loss function is the cost of the error between the prediction g(b) and the observation a at the point b. Loss function is convex function. A convex function shows that there are no local minima. In every optimization problem, the main task is to minimize the loss or cost function. It may be its objective function also. And to minimize the conditional risk, a loss function is derived that is used for outliers.

Typically, a loss function is a value which is based on predicted and true value. And it is the difference between actual and predicted value. Loss function is the penalty for misclassified data points in any classification problem. It is used to analysis the performance of linear regression.

Furthermore, it classifies the data points with high accuracy and it is fit to outliers. Loss function always affects the accuracy. Loss function is convex in nature. Loss function gives two type of error one is positive part error and second is negative part error. Negative part error is always down the accuracy. Proof of its complexity is also explained in proposed methodology chapter.

In binary classification, loss function shows the minimum probability error but from the computational point it is difficult to tackle. Savageboost is faster than other and it is more robust on outliers than others. Moreover it has a faster convergence rate. (8)

Yet, Boosting is gradient decent algorithm. Loss function affects the boosting accuracy. Loss function is convex in nature. Loss function gives two type of error one is positive part error and second is negative part error. Negative part error is always down the accuracy. In this paper positive part truncation is proposed, positive part truncation makes strong to any boosting algorithm Many type of loss function is explained for example hinge loss is used in SVM, exponential loss is used in AdaBoost .It is valid only for global minimization. The loss function which gives local optimization is to be finding out. It increases the adaboost weights and selects the weight which gives minimum error and performance is better than other weights. Gross error sensitivity term is used in this paper Gross error sensitivity is related to outliers. Outliers are the error that is manually created in the dataset. Outliers always decrease the performance. The outliers are increased and performance is noticed on every time. For a given input parameter the conditional probability of class label is known as robust loss function. When sample size become infinite then it became the expected loss function. (9)

Further, output value that is based upon some input parameter is predicted for any classification problem. Relationship between these two is shown by some probability distribution. The main aim of this paper is to find out the classification error probability become very lesser. Classification error will be consistent under some condition and it has a fast convergence rate under less noise condition. Due to non-differentiability, its minimization problem is an N-P hard. Convex function is the base of the boosting algorithm.

In addition, It is based on greedy approach it would stop adding weak classifier when the error become minimum. A boosting algorithm is given for binary classification named direct boost. Ada is work sequential. Error that is given by ensemble classifier is confined by distribution of margin. In this relaxation term is used .Relaxation is used to overcome the problem when it is impossible to maximize the margin along coordinate direction.

After setting the positive and negative relaxation algorithm allow this on a single coordinate to change margin(10).

1.2 Motivation

Boosting is a representation on gradient decent algorithm for loss functions. Loss function maps a real time event to a number representing the cost associated with that event. The goal of any optimization problem is to minimize the loss function as much as possible. Loss function is the penalty for misclassified data points in any classification problem. The main objective of estimation is to find an objective function that models its input well i.e. it should be able to predict the values correctly. The loss function is a measure to quantify the amount of deviation between the predicted values and actual values.

Suppose that $(u_1, v_1), \ldots, (u_n, v_n)$ is observed, where u_i is the value of input space χ and v_i is the class label which takes 1 or -1 value. The collection of weak learners is denoted by $WL = (w_i(u) : \chi \rightarrow (1, -1)|i = (1, \ldots, l))$, where each learner gives class label for the input values. Strong learner SL is made by consolidated weak learners, where SL is given by:

$$SL = \sum_{i=1}^{l} (\alpha_i w_i(u)) \tag{1.1}$$

The loss given by SL over sample (u, v) is $l(-vSL(u))$, where $l: R \rightarrow R$ is continuous and differentiable function except finite points. It is also called growing functions, Loss function is given by:

$$L(SL) = \left(\frac{1}{n}\right) \sum_{i=1}^{n} l(-v_i * SL(u_i)) \tag{1.2}$$

So, in simple term, a loss function is the cost of the error between the prediction $z(b)$ and the observation at the point b. Loss function is convex function. A convex function shows that there are no local minima. In every optimization problem, the main task is to minimize the loss or cost function. And to minimize the conditional risk, a loss function is derived that is used for outliers. When the main objective of the classifier model is to predict a real valued function, the squared loss error function lead to poor accuracy. However, the choice of a particular loss function plays an important role in generalizing the error in regression(11). The loss function is assumed to be directly proportional to the negative log of the residual density. A novel loss function named learned loss function considers this and uses a negative log of the residual density (12). This research work proposes the use of the learned loss function in extreme gradient boosting in modelling of stock markets.

1.3 Problem Statement

The aim of XGBoost is to give almost accurate result on any dataset. Moreover its performance is also much more than existing ones. A lot of research has been done in this context to develop the boosting algorithm. But the majority of research is focused on accuracy problem. Research on boosting algorithm is started in 1989s (11). Later with the development of boosting algorithm Yoav and Schapire give the Adaboost algorithm. In this algorithm, the final prediction is given by weighted average. Moreover the computation process followed by Adaboost is serial. Boosting is a type of ensemble method and another approach in ensemble method is random forest. But it follows the parallel computation process. In XGBoost both things are available one is parallel computation and other is weighted average. The capacity to do parallel computation in one single machine, as well as the implementation of a sparsity aware algorithm makes it 10 times faster than other implementations. XGBoost can costume objective functions and easily handle missing values. It allows to run cross-validation in each iteration of the algorithm. It has achieved state-of-the-art results in several data competitions and it is an end to end developed system. There is a community that improves the algorithm at Distributed (Deep) Machine Learning Community.

Also, we have to gather data with minimum error. And qualitative data is more useful than the quantitative data. Now, when combining the XGBoost with squared logistic loss function, it gives the minimum loss as compared to logistics loss.

1.4 Scope and Main Objectives

1. To increase the confidence of classification points using squared logistic loss (SqLL) function on Extreme Gradient Boosting for large dataset.

2. The main goal is to find out the ajthat minimize the $L(*)$.

1.5 Impact to the Society

Gradient boosting is an important technique in the rapidly growing field known as predictive data modelling and is being applied in a variety of engineering and scientific disciplines such as biology, psychology, medicine, marketing, computer vision, and remote sensing. This research work will be useful for those in the scientific community who gather data and seek tools for analyzing and interpreting data. It will be a valuable reference for scientists in a variety of disciplines and can serve as a reference for pattern recognition, image processing, and remote sensing.

1.6 Organization of the Book

We begin by describing the state-of-the-art in boosting framework, characteristics requirements, various applications, challenges, design, issues and classification of boosting in general for data mining applications in Chapter 1. The rest of the chapters are organized as under:

Chapter 2: In Chapter 2, we present our idea of boosting with the emphasis on literature review of prior work and present a requesting and basic scale of the publically done work that was published in literature concerned to point of the analysis.

Chapter 3: In this part detailed procedure of the proposed work is described along with the proposed algorithm to answer the picked problem. A detailed remark of a current work is likewise explained in this part

Chapter 4: Results are discussed in this chapter with a detailed description of the dataset, its analysis and sampling process.

Chapter 5: In this chapter conclusion of the whole work done for this research work is given and future work associated with the proposed algorithm is given.

CHAPTER II

Literature Review

2.1 History

Boosting is an algorithm that is widely used in machine learning field. Kearns and Valiant (1988, 1989) (12) (13) asked a question Can weak learners consolidated into a strong one? Boosting algorithm is a reply of this question. This reply is given by Robert Schapire's in a 1990 paper. (11) . So Kearns and Valiant has played an important role in the enlargement of boosting. (14).This algorithm fits a weak classifier to weighted versions of the data iteratively. At each iteration, the data is reweighted such that misclassified data points receive larger weights.

In boosting, several weak learners are combined and prediction is given by one strong learner. The final prediction can hence, be made by weighted average or simple average of weak learners. In weighted average, more weight is given to a learner with higher classification accuracy. On the other hand, no weights are allocated to the weak learners in simple average (12) (11).

In boosting system, various weak learners are consolidated and give a strong learner with higher accuracy. Therefore, bias and variance are considered important parameters to measure the accuracy of these algorithms. The better algorithm is the one which provides high bias and low variance.

In the first boosting hypothesis algorithm problem weak learners turns into a strong learner, which give more accuracy than the random guessing (12).

In this development of boosting algorithm is shown .When boosting come in machine learning field, then adaboost come and after that XGboost play an important role in this field. All related information regarding these algorithms is given in the Fig 1 .Finally; boosting became popular algorithm in this field.

The flow chart of history of boosting is given in the Figure 2.

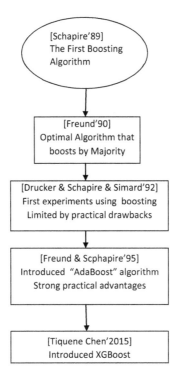

Fig. 1.1 History of Boosting

2.2 XGBoost

XGBoost is also well-known by extreme Gradient Boosting. XGBoost is an extension of gradient boosting by (Friedman, 2001) (Friedman et al., 2000). XGBoost has been successfully used in recent Kaggle competitions, usually as an integral part of the winning ensemble. It implements a variety of Gradient Boosting algorithms, including Generalized Linear Model(GLM) and Gradient Boosted Decision Tree (GBDT). The focus is on scalability. XGBoost differs from Random Forests mainly in the way it creates the tree ensemble. Trees do not have to be trained on a subset of the data or a subset of the features. The ensemble is build sequentially. In each round, k-trees are used to classify examples into k classes. New trees focus on previously misclassified examples to improve the discriminative power of the ensemble.

Boosting increases the risk of overfitting, to prevent this, XGBoost employs early stopping. XGBoost can use any loss function that specifies a gradient. It consists linear model. It also contains tree learning method. It is faster than other because of parallel computation. Regression, classification (15), ranking (16) and in online advertise system (17) etc. Various objective functions are support by XGBoost. In this users can easily define their own objectives. It also has linear model solver algorithm and also this is a package in R version. (18). This package has several features like speed (Due to parallel computation its speed is faster than other algorithm. Moreover its speed is ten times more than gradient boosting method ,input type (in this input may be a dense ,sparse matrix and any local file),execution (XGBoost has better execution on several datasets.) The function of this package has less parameter and it is R friendly function $xgb.train$ is a training function and it receives $xgb.Dmatrix$ object as an input. For the output it requires gradient and second order gradient. It also has row extraction feature that is helpful to find out the cross validation (4).

It is a library designed for boosting trees algorithms. Gradient boosting algorithm is firstly given   by Friedman et al. XGBoost algorithm is nearly related to gradient boosting. Specifically, it is an extension of the classic gbm algorithm .It is also used for supervised learning problems, where we use the training data (with multiple features) x_i to predict a target variable y_i. It is similar to gradient boosting framework but more efficient. It has both linear model solver and tree learning algorithms. This makes XGBoost faster than other. Later it is great in predictive power but relatively slow with implementation, "XGBoost" becomes an ideal fit for many competitions. It also has extra features for cross validation and important variables. In optimization problem many parameters needs to be controlled. XGBoost gives better performance results than Linear Regression or Random Forest Regression. XGBoost is a library designed for tree algorithms. The main goal of this to give a scalable, portable and accurate framework for large scale tree boosting. It is an development on the present Gradient Boosting technique.

Additionally, XGBoost is fast parallel tree. XGBoost handles millions of sample on a single node. XGBoost is a top down approach. The framework defined in this paper can keep running without the support of any current distributed systems. So this system is portable in nature. XGBoost can scale with several specialists easily and take care of machine learning issues include Terabytes of real data. It handle billions of dataset and provide linear speedup with extra machine. This system is twice faster than gbm. In the tree boosting, each node has a duplicacy of the model. If any node get failed then it easily get information from other node. At the point when there are different machines, we can circulate the information by columns, and produce local data block in every machine. In this non continuous memory access process is used. For the splitting process it used a weighted quantile algorithm and when the data is not appropriate in memory then it is divided in to numerous blocks. The records in every chunk is kept in a Compressed Column Storage (CSC) format, with each column arranged by the feature value. (1). The given figure 3 show the XGBoost

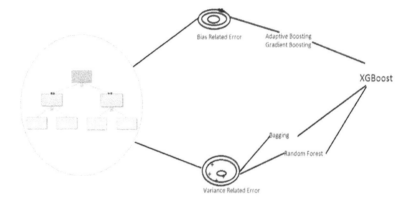

Fig. 2.2 XGBoost

In addition, Sparsity-aware algorithm is works on sparse data. Approximate tree learning works on weighted quantile sketch. Cache access patterns, sharding and data compression are given to make XGBoost scalable .Regularized learning objective is also given for completeness and also it is a end to end system tree boosting system. It can resolve the real world problem with less number of resources. It is scalabe in nature. It handles the sparse data. Its greedy in nature, because it greedily add the trees to perform better result. In this traditional row sub-sampling is also used, and the user says that column sub-sampling is used to remove overfitting problem. Column sub-sampling increase the computational speed. When data is not fit in memory then approximate algorithm is used. (3)

2.3 Random Forest

Random Forests were developed by Leo Breiman. The idea is to create a forest of uncorrelated decision trees. Random Forests combine bagging and random feature selection. The randomness is injected at two stages into the training process. First, each tree is grown on a random subset of the data. The random samples are picked with replacement. This is the bootstrapping part of bagging (short for bootstrap aggregating). Second, at each split only a random subset of the features is used for the decision. Both measures try to avoid highly correlated trees and overfitting. The final prediction is the result of a majority vote over all trees, the aggregating. This mainly reduces the variance and improves the predictive power. Given the random nature of the tree building, there are a lot of trees that aren't particular good. By averaging over the predictions, the hope is that those cancel out. The tree ensembling is embarrassingly parallel. The Random Forest Classifier has been recently used in PConsC2.The tree is constructed using randomness so it called random forest. Regression and classification is done by this ensemble technique. Final prediction is given by simple average. Random forest is a competitor of SVM and boosting. Prediction of both is highly accurate without overfitting. Overfitting problem is controlled by the law of large numbers .Its accuracy depends on the robustness of each classifier. Random selection and random linear combinations is used for inputs. The performance is given by this is paper is similar to the original paper (19).

And, it is also a package that is built in R tool. Random forest is used for classification and regression process. In this number of decision trees are made. The repository that is used for this package is CRAN. It combines two or more ensemble trees into one. Get tree is a function used to extract the information of tree. An integer is a representation of splitting point for any categorical predictors. To add additional tree grow() function is used. Importance of variable is shown by importance() function. It does not handle the missing values. The errors in random forest is plot by plot.randomForest() function. Random forest is applied by randomForest() function. Crossvaliation is shown by rfcv() function (20).Figure 4 show the working of random forest.

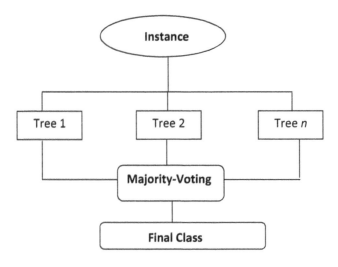

Fig. 2.3 Random Forest

Below mentioned are the notable advantages and disadvantages of Random Forest (21)

Advantages

• It runs effectively on high dataset.

• It can handle a huge number of info factors without variable erasure.

• It gives importance of factors and also tells what factors are essential in the order.

• It is the available algorithm which is highly correctly classifies the data points for many dataset. (22).

• It guesses the missing value and finally maintains accurateness of dataset.

Disadvantages

• The algorithm may become slow if there is huge number of trees.

• It has been seen to overfit for some datasets with noisy classification (23).

2.4 AdaBoost

It executes Freund and Schapire's Adaboost.M1using classification trees as single classifiers. When classifiers are prepared, then they are used to expect on different data. In the ada bag package many function are available. Cross validation function is used to find out the *errors.margin()* is accessible to figure out the margin for these classifiers. Higher flexibility is accomplished offering access to the *rpart.control()*. Four essential new elements were presented on version 3.0, AdaBoost-SAMME (Zhu et al., 2009) is executed and *errorevol()* demonstrates the errors. The "newmfinal" option is used to pruned the ensemble in the *predict.bagging()* and *predict.boosting()*.A probability of every class is get from this that called posterior probability. Version 3.1 changes the relative significance measure to consider the pickup of the Gini index. It is given by a variable in every tree and the weights of these trees..In this there are three new plots i.e. *importanceplot()*, *plot.errorevol()* and *plot.margins()*. Prediction on unlabeled data is also available in Version 4.1. (24)

Likewise, in adaboost weak learner are used to find out weak hypothesis with the minimal weighted error. A number of weak hypothesis are made on numerous of weak learners. The final prediction is given by the combination of these weak hypotheses. Its greedy in nature and it add the weak learner with minimal error. The accuracy of weak hypothesis is superior to random guessing. In paper (6)Vapnik and Chervonenkis theory is applied to adaboost. The training error in adaboost is becomes zero in less iterations. Boosting is a process in which error rate quickly drop down with the increasing the iterations. Adaboost does not fit the overfitting problem in case of margin explanation adaboost will succeed without overfitting. Adaboost gives the exponential loss. Many approaches are used to handle the noise problem and this is also a problem with adaboost. (6)

As well, Boosting is used to increase the performance of base classifier. It consolidates weak rules. The origin of boosting algorithm is given in PAC theory. Its complexity is polynomial in nature. Adaboost is used to diminish the exponential loss. There are three modified adaboost That is real,gentle and logitadaboost. Adabag is an implementation on AdaBoost. Regularization is used to overcome the overfitting problem(25).

Besides this, there is a similarity is given between the adaboost and random forest algorithm. Adaboost algorithm is a successful algorithm while random forest is at least as good algorithm. Adaboost breaks the statistics rules by iteratively fitting on dataset the dataset may be noisy. Adaboost is an optimization and random forest is not work on optimization. It works best when there is large number of trees is available. Adaboost is a part of random forest. Adaboost is only used to overfit problem. After increasing the number of trees the error rate become slow in both cases(26).

2.5 Loss Function

In this section, we will introduce the loss function. The loss function is the measure of prediction accuracy that we define for the problem at hand. We are ultimately interested in minimizing the expected loss, which is known as the risk. The function which minimizes the risk is known as the target function. This is the optimal prediction function we would like to obtain. To minimize the conditional risk, a loss function is derived that is used for outliers. SavageBoost,a new boosting algorithm is also given for minimization of loss. It is less sensitive to the outliers as comparison of logit, Ada, real boost. Minimum conditional risk that is a type of loss function is used to minimize the expected loss. The existing loss function is not sensitive to the outliers (27) and also it has slow convergence. In binary classification these loss function show the minimum probability error but from the computational point it is difficult to tackle. Savageboost is faster than other and it is more robust on outliers than others. Moreover it has a faster convergence rate. (8)

Yet, Boosting is gradient decent algorithm. Loss function affects the boosting accuracy. Loss function is convex in nature. Loss function gives two type of error one is positive part error and second is negative part error. Negative part error is always down the accuracy. In this paper positive part truncation is proposed, positive part truncation makes strong to any boosting algorithm   Many type of loss function is explained for example hinge loss is used in SVM, exponential loss is used in AdaBoost .It is valid only for global minimization. The loss function which gives local optimization is to be finding out. It increases the adaboost weights and selects the weight which gives minimum error and performance is better than other weights. Gross error sensitivity term is used in this paper Gross error sensitivity is related to outliers. Outliers are the error that is manually created in the dataset. Outliers always decrease the performance. The outliers are increased and performance is noticed on every time. For a given input parameter the conditional probability of class label is known as robust loss function. When sample size become infinite then it became the expected loss function. (9)

Further, output value that is based upon some input parameter is predicted for any classification problem. Relationship between these two is shown by some probability distribution. The main goal is to find out the classification error probability become very lesser. Classification error will be consistent under some condition and it has a fast convergence rate under less noise condition. Due to non-differentiability, its minimization problem is an N-P hard. Convex function is the base of the boosting algorithm.

In addition, It is based on greedy approach it would stop adding weak classifier when the error become minimum. A boosting algorithm is given for binary classification named direct boost. Ada is work sequential. Error that is given by ensemble classifier is confined by distribution of margin. In this relaxation term is used .Relaxation is used to overcome the problem when it is impossible to maximize the margin along coordinate direction. After setting the positive and negative relaxation algorithm allow this on a single coordinate to change margin. (10)

CHAPTER III
Proposed Work

3.1 Outline

Data driven Modeling (DDM) encompasses an approach of empirical modeling which involves the analysis of time series data rather than the analysis of the physical processes or the mathematical equations describing the phenomenon. Thus, DDM is a field of mapping the dependent variable on the set of independent variables without the actual knowledge of the physical behavior of the system. In the course of recent decades, DDM has turned out to be one of the backbones of data innovation and with that, a somewhat central, although typically hidden, part of our life. With the constantly expanding amounts of data getting to be noticeably accessible, there is justifiable reason to consider that DDM will turn out to be a significant element for technological advancements. In all aspects of life, application of the same is utilized. Example applications include stock market prediction, credit rating, fraud detection, e-mail protection and recommender system etc.(1). The general approach to modeling involves training the model from known values aiming to minimize the model error, and then predicting the output of unknown variables (Fig.3.1)(2).

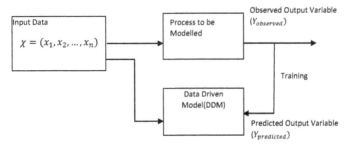

Fig. 3.1 Data Driven Modeling

3.2 Proposed Approach

There aren't as many hyper parameters for Random Forest and XGBoost. A coarse grid search is sufficient. Initial results of Random Forest were nowhere near XGBoost. We also had memory issues and decided to drop the Random Forest in later experiments and focus solely on XGBoost.

The most important parameters of XGBoost are the depth of the trees and the learning rate (eta). Increasing the maximum depth increases the chance of overfitting. The numbers of trees are determined by its round's number. XGBoost can impose an asymmetric error too artificially balance out the data. It made no difference. The final output didn't balance the data and used eta = 1 and a maximum depth of 4.

Gradient boosting is a technique which is used for classification and regression problem. It gives a prediction model in the form of weak prediction models. Boosting is also called an optimization algorithm for a cost function. Like other boosting methods, gradient boosting consolidated weak base into a strong base.

We started with linear regression because it is a really simplest and fastest (in terms of implementation time) model. We can increase number of trees to as much as we want and make it as large as we want only computational time really matters in this case. Fig. 3.2 perfectly describes the decision tree in case of regression problem.

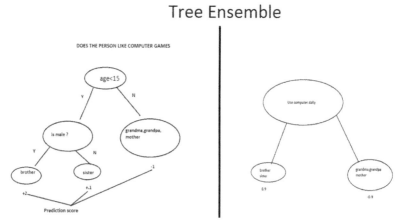

Fig. 3.2 Decision tree of XGBoost library for regression problem

We tried to ensemble different algorithms even if we trained our models based on XGBoost. The first step was to implement very simple model just to have a baseline. We split our training data set in two parts. First part is for training data set and second part is for test training data set. We divide our dataset in to two parts. First, 70% of training set and set this as training set, and 30% as test set. We tried very simple model as a baseline. Without any regularization, since we clearly do not over fit our data. We see that such simple model can't represent our data properly since it lacks features and it separates space badly.

3.2.1 Objective of XGBoost

The objective function of XGboost is defined with respect to 2 terms as given in eq. 3.1.

$$Objective = l(\emptyset) + w(\emptyset) \qquad (3.1)$$

1st term of objective function is training loss function which measures how predictive our model is.

2nd term is regularization term which helps us to overfitting the data.

3.2.2 Parameters

The most important parameters in XGBoost for parameter tuning will be reviewed, as well as the way to tune them.This is a summary of what can be found at Distributed (Deep) Machine Learning Community (2017). The authors define three different groups of parameters for XGBoost set up:

1. General parameters: Parameters to configure the overall algorithm, such as booster type,printed messages and parallel processing.
2. Parameters for Tree Booster: Parameters to configure the booster. Only tree booster parameters will be reviewed because they outperform the linear ones.
3. Learning Task Parameters: Parameters related to the objective function and the evaluation metric.

In this Section only tree booster parameters and learning task parameters will be explained, due to the relevance of their tuning process to produce better predictions.

To have a clear idea before going into details, a XGBoost parameter configuration will look like this:

```
param<-list("objective" = "binary:logistic","eval_metric" =
auc","max_depth"=5,
"eta"=0.2, prediction"=TRUE, "num_parallel_tree"=5)
```

Fig. 3.3 Tree Boosting with XGBoost

3.2.3 Parameters for Tree Booster

This is a summary of the most important parameters for tree learners that must be tuned:

• eta (η): learning rate of the algorithm.

− After each boosting step, the eta shrinks the feature weights to make the boosting more conservative. Range: (0, 1]. Default value: 0.3.

• $gamma$ (γ): minimum split loss reduction.

− It is the minimum loss reduction to make another partition on a leaf node. For bigger

values the algorithm will be more conservative. Range: [0, inf]. Default value: 0.

• $max\ depth$: maximum depth of a tree.

− A lower value prevent overfitting. Higher value could learn relationships specific to the

training data. Range: [0, inf]. Default value: 6.

• $min\ child\ weight$ (h_i): proxy of minimum observation for a child.

− It is the minimum sum required of the Hessian. If the sum is less than the parameter,there will not be further partitioning. Range: [0, inf]. Default value: 1.

• $subsample$: ratio of random samples to be used for training.

− Equivalent of the percentage of random observations collected to grow each tree. Prevents overfitting. Range: [0, 1]. Default value: 1.

• $colsamplebytree$: ratio of columns used to train each tree.

− Equivalent of the percentage of random columns collected to grow trees. Range: (0, 1].

Default value: 1.

• $colsamplebylevel$: ratio of columns used to train each split of a tree.

– Same as before, but the randomization of columns are for each split. Same as Random Forest. Range: (0, 1]. Default value: 1.

• $lambda$ (λ): regularization term on the weights.

– L2 regularization term for the weights. Increasing this value will increase the regularization parameter. Default value: 1.

• $alpha$ (α): regularization term on the weights.

Tree Boosting Data Competitions with XGBoost

– L1 regularization term for the weights. Increasing this value will increase the regularization parameter. Default value: 0.

• $tree\ method$: construction tree algorithm.

– Different split finding algorithms for tree constructing. 'auto' options leverage exact greedy option and approximation depending on the size of the dataset. Choices: 'auto','exact','approx'. Default value: 'auto'.

• $sketcheps$: number of candidates for approximate greedy algorithm.

– This parameter select the number of candidates per feature to be evaluated in each split. This can be translated as 1/sketch eps. Lower values will propose more candidates andbe more accurate. Range: (0, 1). Default value: 0.03.

• $max\ delta\ step\ and\ scale\ pos\ weight$: useful for classes extremely unbalanced.

All the parameters could be found in the package documentation.

3.2.4 Learning Task Parameters

For the learning task parameters there is also a great variety. There are two main parameters with several options: the objective function and the evaluation metric. For the objective function the most commonly used will be described; for the evaluation metric, the ones defined in this research work.

$objective$ (L): definition of the objective function.

– 'reg:linear': linear regression.

– 'reg:logistic': logistic regression.

– 'binary:logistic': logistic regression for binary classification, output probability.

• eval metric ($e(\Theta)$): evaluation metric for the validation data.

– 'rmse': root mean square error.

– 'auc': area under the curve.

• seed: Random seed.

3.2.5 Training & Parameter tuning

Tuning the parameters of an algorithm does not follow a particular methodology. The two elements to take into account are (1) the possible parameters for the algorithm and (2) their performance. Different parameterization of the algorithm must be tested to find their best values in the training set, while avoiding overfitting. To test the different parameter values of the algorithm grid search or random search can be used.

Grid search consists in creating a grid of all the possible/reasonable parameter values for the algorithm. Each row of the grid is a different set up of the parameters and the total of rows is the permutations of all the possible parameter values. Of course, for continuous parameters there is not a way to test all the possible values, but instead either the possible/logical values or their quantiles can be tested. The primary problem of grid search is its computational cost. Random search, as can be inferred, consists in selecting the different parameter values randomly and testing its results. XGBoost package does not have any hyperparameter tuning options; to do this parametric search caret package will be used

As guidance, some modellers use these steps to make parameter tuning for XGBoost:

1. Select a low learning rate $\eta = 0.1$
2. Optimize the parameters of the tree booster:
(a) max depth
(b) colsamplebytree
(c) subsample
3. Aggregate the performance.
4. Tune the regularization parameters, α and λ.
5. Test lower values for η.

Fig. 3.4 XGBoost Parameters

3.2.6 What XGBoost Brings to the Table

All the discussion so far has been general to tree boosting and is therefore relevant for both traditional techniques and XGBoost. In summary, tree boosting is so effective because it fits additive tree models, which have rich representational ability, using adaptively determined neighborhoods. The property of adaptive neighborhoods makes it able to use variable degrees of flexibility in different regions of the input space. Consequently, it will be able to perform automatic feature selection and capture high-order interactions without breaking down. It can thus be seen to be robust to the curse of dimensionality.

XGBoost uses clever penalization of the individual trees. The trees are consequently allowed to have varying number of terminal nodes. XGBoost can shrink them using penalization. The benefit of this is that the leaf weights are not all shrunk by the same factor, but leaf weights estimated using less evidence in the data will be shrunk more heavily. Again, we see the bias-variance trade off being taken into account during model fitting.

Finally, XGBoost includes an extra randomization parameter. This can be used to correlate the individual trees even further, possibly resulting in reduced overall variance of the model. Ultimately, XGBoost can be seen to be able to learn better neighborhoods by using a higher-order approximation of the optimization problem at each iteration. The bias-variance trade off can thus be seen tobe taken into account in almost every aspect of the learning.

3.2.7 Square Logistics Loss Function (SqLL)

In this section, we will introduce the loss function. The loss function is the measure of prediction accuracy that we define for the problem at hand. We are ultimately interested in minimizing the expected loss, which is known as the risk. The function which minimizes the risk is known as the target function. This is the optimal prediction function we would like to obtain.

SqLL holds the property of convexity and convexity means there are no local minima.

$$L(*) = \sum_j [\, (a_j \log_{10}(1 + e^{-a_j})^2 + ((1 - a_j) \log_{10}(1 + e^{a_j}))^2 \,] \tag{3.2}$$

Proof of SqLL convexity is given below

Before starting, convex function can be understood in terms of the following equations:

Convex Function: A function is convex if it satisfies the following condition

$$f(\propto x + (1-\propto)y) \leq \propto f(x) + (1-\propto)f(y)\forall x,y \in Domain\ (f)\ and\ \propto \in [0,1]\ \ (3.3)$$

First order condition for convexity: The condition for first order for convexity is

$$f(y) \geq f(x) + \nabla_x^T f(x)(y-x);\ \ \ \ \ \forall\ x,y\ \in\ Domain(f) \tag{3.4}$$

Second order condition for convexity: The condition for second order for convexity is

$$\forall z\ :\ Z^T\nabla_{x^2}^2 f(x)\ z\ \geq\ 0\ where\ \nabla_x^2\ f(x)\ is\ the\ hessian \tag{3.5}$$

Sum of two convex functions is convex:: Let f(x) and g(x) are two convex function then there are sum is always a convex function.

$$(\varphi_1 f + \varphi_2 g)(x) =\ \varphi_1\ f(x) + \varphi_2\ g(x) \tag{3.6}$$

Proof

$$L(*) = \sum_j [(a_j \log_{10}(1 + e^{-a_j}))^2 + \left((1 - a_j)\log_{10}(1 + e^{a_j})\right)^2] \tag{3.7}$$

Suppose

$$t_\emptyset(x) = \log\ (1 + e^{-\emptyset^i x}) \tag{3.8}$$

Now we have to prove that the following functions are convex in nature and try to prove that it is convex function of $\emptyset$.

$$\log\left(1 + e^{-\Theta^i x}\right) \quad and \quad \log\left(1 + e^{\Theta^i x}\right) \tag{3.9}$$

For this, firstly we have to compute the hessian matrix.

grad:

$$\nabla_\Theta\left[\log\left(1 + e^{-\Theta^T x}\right)\right] = \left(\frac{-e^{-\Theta^i x}}{1 + e^{-\Theta^T x}}\right) x \tag{3.10}$$

$$= \left(\frac{1}{1 + e^{-\Theta^T x}} - 1\right) x \tag{3.11}$$

$$= (h_\Theta(x) - 1) x \tag{3.12}$$

Hessian

$$\nabla_\Theta^2\left[log\left(1 + e^{-\Theta^i x}\right)\right] = \nabla_\Theta\left(\nabla_\Theta\left[log\left(1 + e^{-\Theta^i x}\right)\right]\right) \tag{3.13}$$

CHAPTER IV

Results & Discussions

4.1 Outline

This section details the step-by-step procedure for DDM for stock market prediction using several technical indicators. The model here attempts to forecast the price change of the stocks using the proposed method and a comparison of accuracy is made to evaluate the results and to check the efficacy of the stated approach.

4.2 Dataset

This study uses total ten years of historical data from Jan 2007 to Aug 2017 of two stock market indices CNX Nifty and S&P BSE Sensex which are highly voluminous. All the data is obtained from http://www.nseindia.com/ and http://www.bseindia.com/websites.

4.3 Tools and Platforms

R is an open source distribution system. It is statics software which is easy to use. It is also used for large-scale data processing, predictive analytics, and scientific computing, that aims to simplify package management and deployment. Packages are easily available in this.

4.4 Feature Construction

The first step involves the construction of the features of the dataset to make the predictions of the next day. The 10-year price series of the stock data consists of Date, Open, High, Low, Last and Volume. However the features are evaluated from various technical indicators as below in Table 4.1:

Table 4.1: Feature Construction

Sr. No.	Technical Indicator	Description
1	Force Index(FI)	Indicator to assess the power behind a move
2	William%R	Technical Analysis Indicator to show the current closing price with respect to high and low values of the past n days.
3	Relative Strength Index	Momentum Oscillator to measure the speed and change of price movements
4	Rate of Change(ROC)	Momentum Oscillator to measure the % change of price movements
5	Momentum(MOM)	The difference between current price and previous price

Force Index: This indicator uses the closing price and the volume to assess the power/motive behind the move. Force Index of a single period is evaluated as the difference of the closing price multiplied by the volume. However, FI of more than single period is evaluated as the moving average of the previous periods. It is evaluated as follows, where CP represents the closing price:

$$FI = \big(CP(\text{Current Period}) - CP(\text{Prior Period})\big) * \text{Volume} \qquad (4.1)$$

William Percentage R: This is a technical Analysis Indicator to show the current closing price with respect to high and low values of the past n days. In other words, this represents the momentum oscillator of the stock and is evaluated as following:

$$William\%R = \left(\frac{Highest - close}{Highest - Lowest}\right) * Volume \qquad (4.2)$$

Relative Strength Index(RSI): This is a momentum Oscillator to measure the speed and change of price movements.

$$RSI = 100 - \left(\frac{100}{1 + \frac{Upward\ Price\ Change}{Down\ Price\ Change}}\right) \qquad (4.3)$$

Rate of Change(ROC): This indicator is also an evaluation of the momentum Oscillator to measure the % change of price movements and can be evaluated as follows:

$$ROC = \left(\frac{Current\ Closing\ Price - Closing\ Price\ (Prior\ Period)}{Closing\ Price\ (Prior\ Period)}\right) * 100 \qquad (4.4)$$

Momentum: The technical indicator evaluates the difference between current price and previous price:

$$Momentum = (Current\ Closing\ Price - Previous\ Price\ ) \qquad (4.5)$$

4.5 Feature Selection

Feature selection involves selecting the most relevant features enhancing the accuracy of the predictive model. There are three most widely used categories of feature selection algorithms namely: Filter, Wrapper, and Embedded. In our DDM, the method used is the filter approach which selects the features on the basis of the score generated by a statistical measure. The statistical measure used in our filter method is the mean of the values.

4.6 Training the Model

The model is trained using the proposed XGBoost with Learned Loss(LL) with state of art XGBoost, AdaBoost, AdaBoost-NN, Linear Regression(LR),Neural Network(NN), Decision Tree(DT), Support Vector Machine(SVM), bagging-DT, bagging-NN and Random Forest algorithms. The parameters to be evaluated are accuracy, Type 1 error and Type 2 error (in Percentages). The results are evaluated with the three evaluation techniques explained in section 4.7.

4.7 Evaluation Techniques

Experiments are performed to evaluate the proposed algorithm on the following evaluation techniques: Accuracy using Data splitting (Train/Test Dataset), K-fold Cross Validation, Stratified Cross Validation and Gross Error Sensitivity (18).

4.8 Analysis of Results

1. With Training and Testing Data Set: Here, the dataset is split into two parts: Training and Testing set, The size of training set taken is 67%, whereas that of testing is 33%. The method is used in case of large datasets and produces performance estimates with lower bias. Table 4.2 shows that the proposed method outperforms other algorithms by huge margin:

Table 4.2: Comparative Evaluation of Boosting Algorithms

Boosting Technique	Accuracy(%)	Type I error(%)	Type II error(%)
XGBoost with LL	**89.92**	12.67	11.61
XGBoost	87.81	13.92	**10.80**
AdaBoost	85.64	17.40	11.93

AdaBoost-NN	84.95	14.12	16.23
LR	86.67	**8.67**	16.88
NN	85.05	12.06	16.87
DT	84.42	17.36	13.95
SVM	85.54	15.35	13.72
Bagging-DT	86.42	13.33	13.78
Bagging-NN	85.62	11.83	16.42
Random Forest	86.34	13.42	14.39

2. K-Fold Cross Validation Method: This cross validation method is used to evaluate the performance of XGBoost on the new data with k set to 3,5,or 10. Here, the data is divided into K folds. After evaluating the techniques on different k performance scores, the results are averaged out. This is a more reliable way to measure the performance of the algorithm.

Table 4.3: Comparison of Boosting Techniques using K-Fold Cross Validation

Boosting Technique	Accuracy(%)	Type I error(%)	Type II error(%)
XGBoost with LL	**77.98**	33.62	**9.35**
XGBoost	76.69	34.87	23.46
AdaBoost	61.25	40.18	37.32
AdaBoost-NN	64.09	33.61	38.22
LR	64.74	41.37	29.14

NN	63.65	35.22	40.49
DT	60.11	46.03	33.74
SVM	60.67	41.29	37.36
Bagging-DT	62.43	37.43	37.71
Bagging-NN	65.34	34.07	35.25
Random Forest	66.25	**30.90**	36.50

3. Stratified Cross Validation: The method is particularly applicable when the categories are large and there is imbalance in the instances of each category. In this method, stratified folds are created when performing the cross validation which in a way creates the effect of enforcing the uniform distribution of classes in each fold as the distribution is in the whole training dataset. Table 4.4 shows the accuracy achieved from XGBoost with LL is 77.34%.

Table 4.4: Comparison of Boosting Techniques using Stratified Cross Validation

Boosting Technique	Accuracy(%)	Type I error(%)	Type II error(%)
XGBoost with LL	**77.34**	23.71	10.71
XGBoost	76.95	23.74	19.37
AdaBoost	73.61	26.57	13.46
AdaBoost-NN	73.75	29.95	16.09
LR	76.43	12.46	11.28
NN	72.54	30.13	17.75

DT	72.65	29.37	13.63
SVM	76.07	33.73	**6.88**
Bagging-DT	75.19	28.19	10.51
Bagging-NN	76.01	**9.67**	12.98
Random Forest	76.59	11.37	11.42

4. Error Graph: The error graph of random forest is given in figure 4.1,adaboosterror graph is given in figure 4.2 and XGBoost error graph is given in figure 4.3.

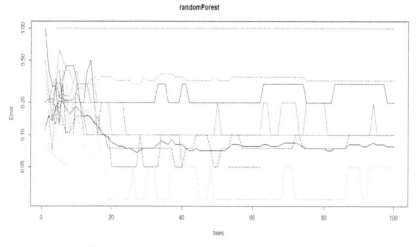

Fig. 4.1 Error result of Random Forest on different classes

Ensemble error vs number of trees

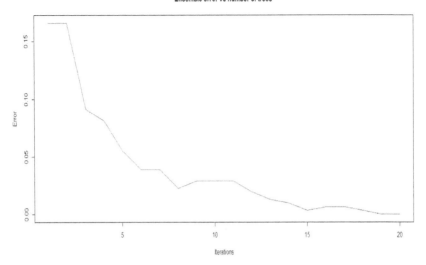

Fig. 4.2 Ensemble error vs. number of trees in AdaBoost

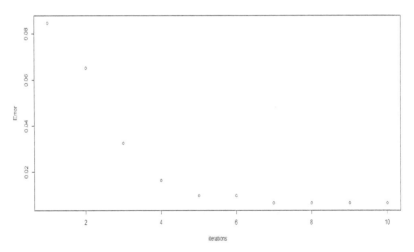

Fig. 4.3 XGBoost Error graph vs. number of iterations

CHAPTER V
Summary, Recommendations, and Future Directions

5.1 Overview

Boosting Calculation is a standout amongst the most intense learning thoughts presented over the most recent twenty years. It was intended for problems related to data classification; however it can be stretched out to relapse too. The inspiration for Extreme Gradient Boosting was a strategy. That consolidates the yields of many "weak" classifiers to deliver a strong classifier. A weak classifier (e.g. decision tree) is one whose error rate is just superior to anything irregular speculating. This Chapter presents the overall discussion of the study. It covers on inferences gathered from experiments conducted, problems that occurred during study, advantages and limitations from the study, and scope for future research. The explicit contributions of the book are summarized in the following section 5.2.

5.2 Summary

We saw that boosting algorithm is very vast in itself and also it has many interpretations. AdaBoost is better than a random imagination and also we saw that XGBoost has a fast performance due to parallel computation while other boosting algorithm works on serial computations. Missing values is handled in these algorithms. Over fitting problem is also overcome by these algorithms. In boosting system, various weak learners are consolidated and give a strong learner with higher accuracy. The better algorithm is the one which provides high bias and low variance. Both XGBoost and AdaBoost depict the same. But Random forest shows the opposite. Accuracy is also impacted by the cross validation of error. All the three algorithms implement the cross validation of error and hence are more accurate than single learner. To state the comparative analysis of the accuracy of all the six algorithms, accuracy of XGBoost is maximum and random forest shows the least accuracy amongst all. Over fitting of data occurs due to the branches involving noisy data or outliers. It is imperative to reduce the overfitting problem to enhance the accuracy of the learners. Pruning is done to remove the overfitting of data. The pruning can be done in two ways: Pre pruning and post pruning. Prepruning involves the avoidance of overfitting problem while post pruning removes the overfitted data after the learner is created. XGBoost and Random Forest avoids overfitting problem, Adaboost does not avoid the problem completely but it is less prone to overfitting.

Moreover ,A lot of analysis was performed on the data toidentify patterns and outliers which would boostor delay the prediction algorithm. Data Mining methods like AdaBoost, Random Forest Regression andXGBoost were implemented and their results compared. XGBoost which is an improved gradientboosting algorithm was observed to perform the best at prediction.

Further, when we apply SqLL on these algorithms then random forest gives better result than the Xgboost and adaboost.It shows minimum loss.

In summary, XGBoost which is implemented on gradient boosting algorithm and follows the greedy approach is best performing boosting algorithm in terms of computation performance and accuracy. In short, performance of Xgboost is better than other boosting algorithm. And after applying SqLL Random forest shows best result other than two.

The comparison between the aforementioned algorithms is done on the basis of computation performance, final prediction, training and testing algorithm, bias and variance. Final prediction can either be made by weighted average or simple average. Similarly, computation process can either be serial or parallel. Further, the algorithms are also related on the basis of whether a control mechanism for over fitting problem is furnished in the algorithm or not. Likewise the algorithm is classified on the basis of training and testing algorithm used in the corresponding boosting algorithm.

5.3 Recommendations

- The proposed XGBoost algorithm addresses the adaptive behavior of algorithm with improved energy efficiency, making it appropriate for the volatile operating conditions. Thence, the proposed algorithm is recommended in place of fixed classification strategies for the dynamic behavior of data mining applications leading to resource savings.
- The results establish that the proposed method attains higher accuracy with the same computational complexity. To that end, the proposed strategy should be preferred in data mining applications with prescribed complexity constraints.

- The study in the case of Squared Logistic Loss Function ascertains that there is considerable improvement in the accuracy, error rate, stability, and bias-variance trade-off in comparison to other ensemble techniques. Therefore, it is suggested that SQLL should be preferred over other loss function for the applications that require higher accuracy..
- The proposed strategy SQLL based boosting can be treated as groundwork for innovative adaptive solutions considering another category of Classification algorithms well such as, ensemble techniques.

5.4 Future Research Directions

Despite massive research efforts made in the area of ensemble techniques, there are a number of issues that still need to be addressed. In this research work, we have focused on a few aspects of data mining applications for stock forecasting applications. Also, we have proposed a Squared Logistic Loss function based Extreme Gradient Boosting. Nevertheless, there are many issues related to the field of data mining that need to be addressed for further research. These are summarized as follows:

- Traditional classification algorithms expect that the entire training set can reside into the primary memory. As automatic data collection turns into day to day practice in numerous organizations, vast amount of data that surpass the memory limit end up accessible to the learning classifiers. This gives rise to the utilization of scalability in the classification algorithms.
- Beforehand, the investigation of classification techniques concentrated on investigating different learning mechanisms to enhance the accuracy on unobserved cases. In any case, recent investigation on imbalanced data sets has shown that accuracy is not a proper measure to assess the performance of a classification algorithm when the data set is to a great degree uneven, in which every one of the illustrations belong to at least one, bigger classes and far less cases belong to a smaller, typically more intriguing class. Since numerous real world data sets are unbalanced, there has been a pattern toward adjusting present classification algorithms to better identify examples in the uncommon class.

- The ensemble can be obtained selective combination of ensemble members using several optimization techniques e.g. hill climbing techniques to selectively regulate the classifiers of the ensemble to combine by calculating various parameters based on accuracy or diversity.
- Heterogeneous ensemble techniques can be investigated by combing different kind of classifiers rather than a single class of classifiers combined together.

References

1. XGBoost: Reliable large-scale tree boosting system. **Chen and Guestrin, Carlos.** San Francisco, CA, USA : s.n., 2016. Proceedings of the 22nd SIGKDD Conference on Knowledge Discovery and Data Mining.

2. "A Short Introduction to Boosting". **Freund and Schapire.** 1999.

3. "Xgboost: A scalable tree boosting system." . **Chen, Tianqi and Guestrin, Carlos** . s.l. : 22Nd ACM SIGKDD International Conference on Knowledge Discovery and Data Mining. ACM, 2016. 22Nd ACM SIGKDD International Conference on Knowledge Discovery and Data Mining. ACM.

4. "xgboost: eXtreme Gradient Boosting." R package version 0.4-2 . **Chen, Tianqi and Tong He.** 2015.

5. ada: An r package for boosting. **Culp, et al., et al.** 2006, Journal of Statistical Software 17.2.

6. "Explaining adaboost.". **Schapire and E, Robert** . Berlin Heidelberg : s.n., 2013. Empirical inference. Springer. pp. 37-52.

7. "The random subspace method for constructing decision forests.". **Ho and Kam, Tin.** s.l. : IEEE transactions on pattern analysis and machine intelligence, 1998.

8. "On the design of loss functions for classification: theory, robustness to outliers, and savageboost". **Masnadi, Shirazi, Hamed and Vasconcelos, Nuno.** s.l. : Advances in neural information processing systems, 2009.

9. "The most robust loss function for boosting." . **Kanamori, Takafumi, et al.** Berlin/Heidelberg : Neural Information Processing. Springer, 2004.

10. "Direct 0-1 loss minimization and margin maximization with boosting.". **Zhai, Shaodan and al., et.** s.l. : Advances in Neural Information Processing Systems, 2013.

11. "The Strength of Weak Learnability" . **Schapire and E., Robert** . s.l. : Machine Learning. Boston, MA: Kluwer Academic Publishers, 1990.

12. Thoughts on Hypothesis Boosting. **Kearns, Michael.** s.l. : 1988.

13. "Crytographic limitations on learning Boolean formulae and finite automata". . **Kearns, Michael and Valiant, Leslie** . s.l. : Symposium on Theory of computing. ACM, 18 January 2015.

14. "Arcing classifier ". **Schapire and Breiman, Leo.** s.l. : Ann. Stat, 2017.

15. Robust Logitboost and adaptive base class (ABC) Logitboost. **Li., P.** s.l. : Twenty-Sixth Conference Annual Conference on Uncertainty in Artificial Intelligence (UAI'10), 2010.

16. "From ranknet to lambdarank to lambdamart: An overview". **Burges and JC, Christopher.** s.l. : Learning 11.23-581, 2010.

17. Practical lessons from predicting clicks on ads at facebook. **He, Xinran, et al., et al.** s.l. : Eighth International Workshop on Data Mining for Online advertising,ADKDD, 2014.

18. Package 'xgboost'. **Chen, Tianqi and He, Tong.** 2017.

19. "Analysis of a random forests model" . **Biau and GÃŠrard.** s.l. : Journal of Machine Learning Research, 2012.

20. Package'randomForest'. **Breiman, Leo and al., et.** s.l. : http://stat-www. berkeley. edu/users/breiman/RandomForests, 2011.

21. "A SURVEY ON INFORMATION MANAGEMENT IN RANDOM FOREST". **Kalokhe, Priyadarshani and Warpe, Kanchan.** s.l. : International Journal of Computer Engineering and Applications, 2013.

22. "An empirical evaluation of supervised learning in high dimensions". **Caruana, Rich, Karampatziakis, Nikos and Yessenalina, Ainur.** s.l. : 25th International Conference on Machine Learning (ICML), 2008.

23. Machine Learning Benchmarks and Random Forest Regression. **Segal and R. , Mark.** s.l. : Center for Bioinformatics & Molecular Biostatistics., April 14 2004.

24. "Package 'adabag'.". **Alfaro, Esteban and al, et.** s.l. : ufpr.br, 2015.

25. "Adabag: An R package for classification with boosting and bagging.". **Alfaro, et al., et al.** s.l. : Journal of Statistical Software , 2013.

26. "Explaining the success of adaboost and random forests as interpolating classifiers" . **Wyner, J., Abraham and et al.** s.l. : arXiv preprint arXiv, 2015.

27. "Robust truncated-hinge-loss support vector machines," . **Wu, Y. and Liu, Y.** s.l. : JASA, 2007.

28. Ensemble Methods: Foundations and Algorithms. **Hua, Zhou Zhi.** s.l. : Chapman and Hall/CRC. p. 23. ISBN 978-1439830031, 2012.

29. "Learning with noisy labels". **Natarajan, Nagarajan and al., et.** s.l. : Advances in neural information processing systems, 2013.

30. "Robust and accurate shape model fitting using random forest regression voting.". **Cootes, F.,Tim and al., et.** Berlin Heidelberg : European Conference on Computer Vision. Springer , 2012.

31. "Explaining adaboost." . **Schapire, Robert E.** s.l. : Empirical inference,Springer, 2013. Berlin Heidelberg.